The Gruesome Truth About

The Greeks

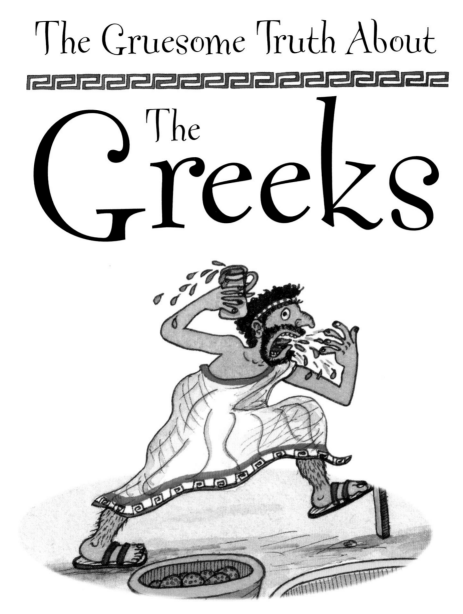

Written by

Jillian Powell

Illustrated by

Matt Buckingham

WINDMILL BOOKS
New York

Published in 2011 by Windmill Books, LLC
303 Park Avenue South, Suite #1280, New York, NY 10010-3657

First Edition

Senior Editor: Claire Shanahan
Design Manager: Paul Cherrill
Designers: Fiona Grant, Jason Billin
Consultant: Anne Millard
Indexer: Cath Senker

Library of Congress Cataloging-in-Publication Data

Powell, Jillian.
 The Greeks / by Jillian Powell. — 1st ed.
     p. cm. — (The gruesome truth about)
 Includes index.
 ISBN 978-1-61533-218-2 (library binding)
 1. Greece—Civilization—To 146 B.C. I. Title.
 DF77.P69 2011
 938—dc22

                                    2010024574

Manufactured in China

For more great fiction and nonfiction,
go to www.windmillbooks.com

CPSIA Compliance Information: Batch #WAW1102W: For Further Information
contact Windmill Books, New York, New York on 1-866-478-0556.

Contents

The Great Greeks

Ancient Greece was a rich and powerful **civilization** that created ideas and designs we still use today. The ancient Greeks lived from around 3000 to 140 BCE, when they were conquered by the Romans.

The Greeks lived in city-states such as Athens, Thebes, and Corinth, which stretched from the Greek mainland and islands to parts of Turkey and Bulgaria. These city-states had their own rulers, laws, and armies.

The Greeks were farmers, traders, soldiers, architects, and engineers. There were also many great poets, playwrights, **philosophers**, and artists.

The Greeks invented **democracy** and modern medicine. Their temple architecture inspired buildings in many of the world's most important cities.

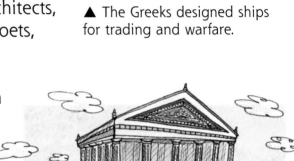

▲ The Greeks designed ships for trading and warfare.

▲ The Parthenon in Athens is the most famous Greek temple. It was built for the goddess Athena between 447 and 438 BCE.

▲ The Olympic games were first held in Greece.

▶ The Greeks are famous for their beautiful temples, theaters, and statues.

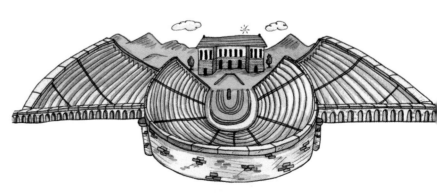

4

Gruesome Truth

Those are some of the things that you probably already know about the Greeks, but in this book, you'll find out the gory and grisly bits that no one ever tells you! Each double page will begin with a well-known FACT, before going on to tell you the gruesome truth about the Greeks. Look for these features throughout the book—the answers are on page 32.

WHAT IS IT?
Guess the mystery object.

TRUE OR FALSE?
Decide if the statement is fact or fiction.

Animal Sacrifices

Temples housed statues of the gods and treasures offered to them, but they were also places of animal sacrifice.

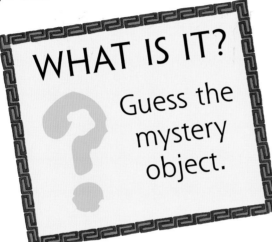

▶ Priests threw barley over the animal and slit its throat at an altar outside the temple.

Games and Gore

FACT The Olympic games began in ancient Greece over 2,500 years ago.

Gruesome Truth

Some of the sports allowed kicking, punching, breaking fingers, and dislocating limbs!

Noisy and Naked

The Olympic games were held in honor of the god Zeus. They attracted huge, noisy crowds. On the third day, a hundred oxen were sacrificed for the god.

Only men were allowed to compete and for most sports, they had to be naked.

▲ The statue of Zeus at the Greek city of Olympia was over 40 feet (12 meters) high.

▲ Any married women found watching the games could be executed.

Violent Victories

The most violent sport was the pankration, or "complete victory" contest. Competitors could do anything they wanted to bring down their opponent, except biting or gouging out eyes. The Spartans did allow that!

▼ Judges stood by holding a stick. They used it to separate the fighters or stop them from cheating.

Boxing and Beatings

Other popular combat sports were wrestling and boxing. Boxers wore leather bands around their wrists and some added sharp spikes!

Anyone who cheated in a sport was punished with a beating or paying a fine. The money was used to pay for statues to the god Zeus.

Fit for Fighting

Fitness was important to young men who might be drafted to be soldiers. Athletes had to prove they had been training for ten months before the games.

▲ One race had to be run in full armor. Competitors ran four lengths of the stadium in armor weighing up to 60 pounds (27 kilograms)!

Champs and Trainers

Most athletes worked with personal trainers. Some ate all-meat diets to build up their body weight and muscle. They sometimes **detoxed** their bodies by making themselves vomit.

Wrestling champ Milo the Giant won six Olympic games. He ate 40 pounds (18 kilograms) of meat and bread and drank 2.5 gallons (10 liters) of wine a day.

WHAT IS IT?

◄ Milo once carried a four-year-old bull around the stadium before eating it!

Stadium Spills

Chariot racing was also a dangerous sport. As many as 40 chariots raced together and there were often crashes and injuries.

TRUE OR FALSE?
The Greeks held games at funerals.

▶ In one race, charioteers had to jump off and on to moving chariots. There were frequent accidents and even deaths.

Grasshoppers and Goats' Cheese

FACT Most Greeks ate a diet of barley bread and porridge, with olives, figs, goats' cheese, squid, and octopus.

Gruesome Truth

At feasts, the rich ate roasted songbirds, grasshoppers, snails, snakes, and **sea urchins**.

Party Menus

Some dinner parties had up to 12 courses! The menu might include:

▲ The Greeks liked eating female grasshoppers when they had mated, because then they were full of eggs.

Menu

Roast turtledove

Piglet stuffed with thrush

Peacock eggs

Fattened snails

Iris bulbs in vinegar

Sacrifices and Soups

Roasted meat was served when an animal had been sacrificed to the gods. The Greeks ate pigs, sheep, goats, deer, donkeys, and hares. Some doctors even recommended puppy meat.

Greek cooks boiled the brains and stuffed the bladder with blood and fat before roasting it. They also roasted the heart, lungs, liver, and kidneys.

People mostly ate with their hands, or used bread to scoop up thick soups.

▼ Bread was sometimes thrown on the floor for dogs to eat, or slaves to clear up later!

▲ The Spartans made a "black soup" that contained salt, vinegar, and boiled pigs' blood.

Slaves and Masters

FACT In ancient Greece, slaves could be teachers, nurses, accountants, and secretaries. They even manned the police force in Athens, where one in three people was a slave.

Gruesome Truth

Masters treated slaves as their property and punished them by starving or beating them. Runaways were branded with a hot iron if they were caught. Slaves could not use their own names, go to school, marry, or have children without their master's agreement.

▲ Slaves were punished for being disobedient.

▼ Slaves had to have bare feet to show they were not free citizens.

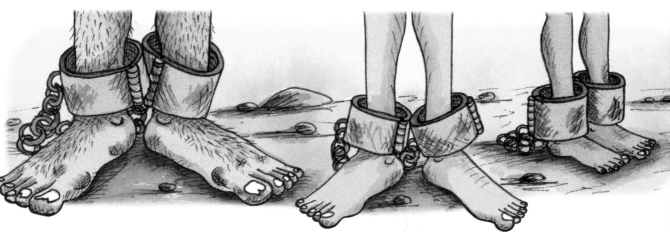

Born and Bought

Some people were born into slavery, others were taken as prisoners of war in battle. Some had been sold by their own parents or became slaves when they were abandoned as babies. Families that could not afford to bring up babies just left them outside the city gates. Sometimes, they were rescued and brought up as slaves. Slaves were bought and sold at markets.

▼ Young, good-looking, and strong slaves went for the best prices. Prices sometimes fell if a battle brought a lot of prisoners of war to the slave market.

TRUE OR FALSE?
Slaves could not go to the bathroom without asking their master's permission.

Jobs and Chores

The luckiest slaves were public slaves employed by the government as clerks or bankers. Private slaves could also be well treated as household servants. Some houses had up to 20 slaves doing the chores.

Ships and Mines

The worst jobs for slaves were working on the ships or in the mines.

Some slaves had to row trading ships. They never saw the sun and were fed on bread and water. Most died young.

Slaves who refused to work or who ran away from their masters might be sent to work in the mines. Around 30,000 slaves worked in the silver mines at Laurion. They lived in **squalor** and worked underground ten hours a day, wearing iron rings around their ankles. Some were criminals, thieves, or murderers. One in four died every year, and most only survived two or three years because the **silver ore** contained poisonous lead, which they breathed in.

▲ The only light the slaves had in the mines was from dirty oil lamps.

▲ On trading ships, a slave master lashed the slaves with a whip to make them row faster.

Healing and Humors

FACT The Greek physician Hippocrates (460–377 BCE) was the founder of modern medicine.

Gruesome Truth

To find out what was wrong with patients, Hippocrates tested samples of their earwax, vomit, pee, tears, or snot.

WHAT IS IT?

▲ Hippocrates tested the patients' samples by tasting them!

Prayers and Charms

Before Hippocrates, the Greeks thought sickness was a punishment from the gods. They prayed and made offerings to the gods to make them better. They carried around bits of bone as lucky charms to keep sickness away.

Blood and Bile

Greek medicine was based on the idea of four "humors": blood, black **bile**, yellow bile, and **phlegm**. They had to be kept in balance for good health.

A fever meant a patient had too much blood. Doctors cut their skin and used leeches to suck the blood out, or a hot cup that drew blood out from a wound as it cooled.

▲ "Cupping" blood was thought to restore the body's balance.

Deadly Dissection

Doctors learned about disease by cutting up dead bodies. They also cut up live apes, dogs, and pigs. One doctor, Herophilus (335–280 BCE), cut up bodies of live criminals to study how their organs worked.

◄ Animals such as apes were used for medical research.

Surgeons could set broken or dislocated bones. They used bone drills to drill into skulls to try and cure headaches or take fluids out of the brain.

They used herbs as **antiseptics**, but many patients died from infections after surgery.

▲ Slipped discs were treated by standing on the patient's back!

Seers and Superstitions

FACT The Greeks believed that the gods sent them **omens**. Trained priests called **seers** could "read" them to tell the future.

Gruesome Truth

Priests sacrificed animals outside of temples, then looked for omens in their livers or guts.

Armies and Omens

Greek armies traveled with their own seers. They sacrificed animals before battles to get omens from the gods.

▶ A healthy liver meant success in battle, but a diseased or funny-shaped liver warned of defeat!

▼ The Greeks also read omens in thunder and lightning, the pattern birds made in flight, and the sound the wind made in trees.

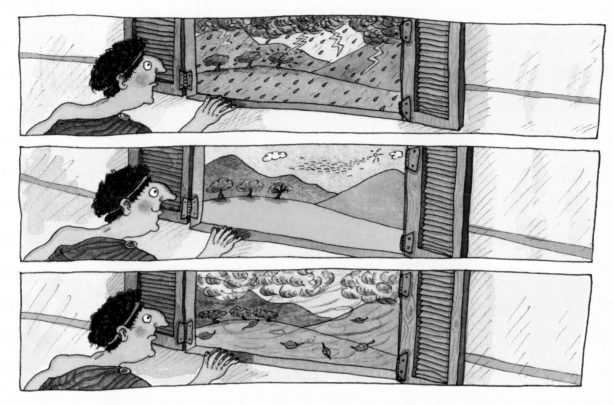

Spirits and Oracles

The ancient Greeks were very **superstitious**. They believed the gods could bless or curse them, so they tried to please them with offerings of money, gifts, or sacrificed animals.

They went to holy places called **oracles** to ask the gods for advice. At the oracle in Corinth, they heard the god's voice booming out from under their feet. In fact, a priest had crept along a secret tunnel that led under the altar, so they heard his voice coming from underground!

As well as angry gods, the Greeks feared bad spirits called keres. They believed they escaped from burial jars to haunt the living. They thought they caused nightmares and even diseases.

▶ People painted tar around their door frames to catch the spirit, so they could get a priest to **exorcise** it.

Bug Bombs and Flamethrowers

FACT Warfare was part of life in ancient Greece, as states fought against each other and enemy states such as the Persians and the Romans.

Gruesome Truth

The Greeks laid **siege** to cities to capture them. If the people inside held out, they poisoned their water, destroyed their crops, and attacked them with flamethrowers, giant catapults, and "bug bombs."

Scorpions and Spears

Bug bombs were clay pots filled with **scorpions** that were dropped on enemy heads. Scorpions were so feared that they were used to decorate the shields of Greek soldiers called **hoplites**. Soldiers also fought with spears and short swords.

TRUE OR FALSE?
Greek heroes used the first biological weapons.

▲ Mice, **hornets**, and gadflies were used in bug bombs, as well as scorpions.

Towers and Tactics

When the Greeks wanted to capture a city, they surrounded it and destroyed crops to starve the enemy out of hiding. They used siege towers on wheels so they could push them right up to the city walls. Then they attacked with crossbows and battering rams.

▲ Poisonous plants such as **hellebores** were used to poison the water in rivers and springs.

They also used giant catapults that fired arrows, javelins, or rocks, and flamethrowers. These were made from hollow tree trunks with a **bellows** at one end that lit an explosive mixture of hot coals, tar, and sulfur.

▼ Flamethrowers sprayed jets of fire at the enemy.

▲ To attack, they used towers to climb the city walls.

Trained Fighters

Many Greek men had to become soldiers to fight for their state. They even had to pay for their own uniform!

In Sparta, children learned to fight from the age of 12. They had to bath in icy water and sleep on rushes, and they were beaten if they disobeyed orders.

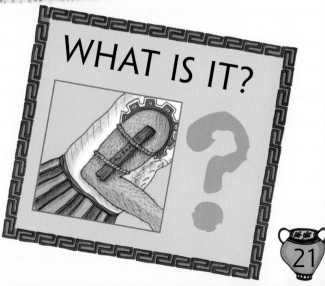

WHAT IS IT?

Warships and Death Rays

FACT The Greeks built fast warships called **triremes**. They were powered by sail and three rows of oarsmen.

Gruesome Truth

Greek warships had bronze battering rams at the bows to crush and sink enemy ships.

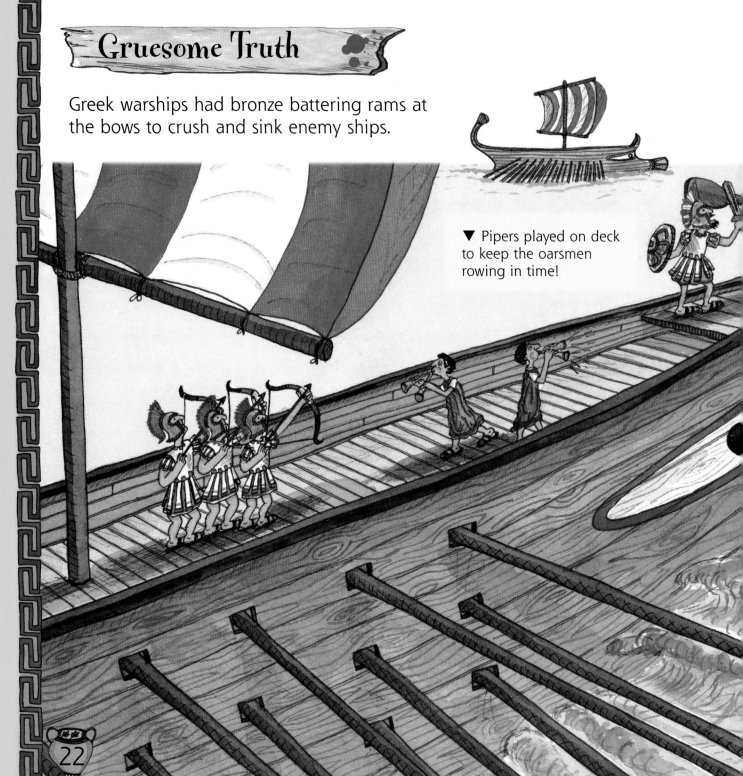

▼ Pipers played on deck to keep the oarsmen rowing in time!

Eyes and Enemies

The warships also had giant eyes painted on the sides to protect the ship from the **Evil Eye** while it was at sea, and frighten the enemy!

The three decks of oarsmen rowed as fast as they could to ram enemy ships in the side. Once a ship had been rammed, archers fired arrows at the enemy crew.

Flaming Weapons

The Greeks used weapons called death rays, invented by **Archimedes** (c. 287–212 BCE). These were probably giant mirrors that reflected the sun's rays onto enemy ships to set them on fire.

◀ Giant catapults fired rocks or javelins at approaching enemy ships.

▶ Death rays were used to defend Syracuse against the Romans in 211 BCE.

23

Pyres and Plagues

FACT Many people died young in ancient Greece. Families and friends gave the dead grand funerals.

Gruesome Truth

Many men died fighting in wars, and many women died in childbirth. Other people died from the **plague** and a variety of other diseases.

▶ Old or sick slaves could be thrown out by their masters and left to perish.

Bodies and Burials

Dead bodies were laid out and washed in seawater. They were buried outside the city walls or burned on piles of wood called funeral pyres that were open to the air.

Mourners wore black clothes. Women cut off their hair, beat their chests, and scratched their faces until the blood ran to show how upset they were.

▼ Babies and children were sometimes buried in big, clay burial jars.

◀ Some families paid for extra mourners to weep and wail at funerals.

The Underworld

The Greeks believed the dead went to the Underworld, called Hades. First, they had to pay the boatman Charon to cross the Styx river. A coin was placed in the mouth after someone died to pay for the river crossing. Then, they had to get past a three-headed dog named Cerberus that guarded the entrance to the Underworld.

▲ Cerberus allowed spirits of the dead to enter but never leave Hades.

The Greeks believed that if they had lived good lives, they went to lovely, sunny fields. But if they had done bad things, they were tortured forever in a deep, gloomy dungeon. Those that were neither good nor bad went to fields where they just drifted and faded away!

Ruthless Rulers

FACT The Greeks began the idea of democracy, giving citizens the power to vote for their rulers.

Gruesome Truth

Only men over 30 who were landowners were allowed to vote. No women, foreigners, slaves, or poor people could vote!

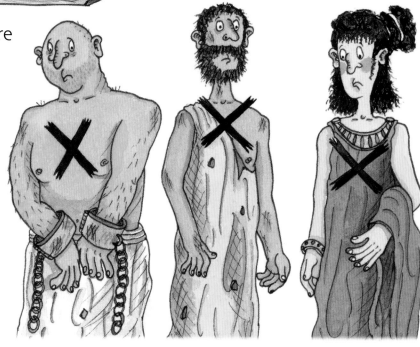

▶ Many people in ancient Greece had no political rights or citizenship.

Votes and Punishments
Men voted for rulers in their city-state, but could also vote for people they wanted to send into **exile**. They wrote their names on pieces of broken pottery, and if anyone got over 6,000 votes, he had to leave the state.

States kept their own strict laws. Athens and Sparta had some of the toughest laws. Death or exile were common punishments.

Draco's Laws
One of the first rulers of Athens was Draco (c. 659–601 BCE). His laws were so strict that people said he wrote them in blood—not ink! Draco believed all crimes should be punished with death.

▼ Under Draco's laws, you could be sentenced to death for stealing an apple or a cabbage, or for just being lazy!

Courts and Criminals

Criminals were judged by a jury in a court. Most trials were completed in just one day.

If a woman was the victim of a crime, she could not go to court herself, but had to send a male relative to represent her. Slaves were often tortured to give evidence.

In Sparta, children caught stealing were given a beating. But they were often starved of food so they would learn skills such as stealing! They were beaten in front of temple altars to show how strong and brave they were. Some bled to death.

WHAT IS IT?

▶ If someone owed you money, you had the power to make him or her your slave.

Myths and Monsters

FACT The Greeks told many **myths** and legends about gods, heroes, and monsters, which poets wrote down in great poems and histories.

Gruesome Truth

Greek myths tell of hideous man-eating monsters and grisly deaths. Even Greek gods could be jealous and cruel.

Deadly Deities

Anyone who angered or upset the gods would be horribly punished. Marysas was a **satyr** who dared to challenge the god Apollo to a flute-playing contest. When Apollo won, he had Marysas skinned alive as punishment. When a **nymph** named Echo rejected the god Pan, he had her torn apart by shepherds, leaving only her voice.

▲ The goddess Circe was so jealous of a nymph's beauty, she threw magic herbs into a pool where she was bathing. Six heads sprang out of the nymph's neck, each one with three rows of teeth!

28

▼ The monsters called Harpies had the faces of old women and the bodies of birds with long claws.

▼ The Cyclops were giants with one eye in the middle of their forehead.

▼ The Sphinx had the head of a woman and the body of a lion. She stopped travelers on the road to Thebes and asked them a riddle. If they got the answer wrong, she strangled them with her serpent's tail, then ate them.

▼ The Minotaur was half-man, half-bull. It lived in an underground maze called a **labyrinth** on the Greek island of Crete. Every year, it had to be fed seven boys and seven girls from Athens.

Glossary

antiseptic	A substance used to clean wounds.
Archimedes	A famous mathematician and inventor who lived 287–212 BCE.
bellow	A device that blows air.
bile	A greenish liquid that is made by the liver.
civilization	A people or culture with wealth and learning.
democracy	A type of government in which people can vote for their ruler.
detox	To work out the toxins or poisons from a body.
Evil Eye, the	A belief in people or looks that have the power to curse.
exile	To force out of a place or country.
exorcise	To drive out a bad spirit.
hellebore	A flowering plant, of which some species are poisonous.
hoplite	A foot soldier who wore armor.
hornet	A large type of wasp.
labyrinth	An underground maze.
mourner	A person who is grieving for someone who has died.
myth	An old story and belief passed down through the ages.
nymph	A young girl who is a minor goddess in Greek and Roman mythology.
omen	A sign that points to future events.
oracle	A place where people went to ask questions about the future.
philosopher	A great thinker.
phlegm	Sticky mucus.
plague	A disease that spreads and kills people.
satyr	A creature in Greek mythology that was half man and half goat.
scorpion	An insectlike creature of the spider family with a sting in its tail.
sea urchin	A sea creature with a spiny shell.
seer	Someone who can tell the future by seeing signs in nature.
siege	A technique of surrounding and attacking.
silver ore	The rock from which silver can be extracted.
squalor	Dirty and miserable conditions.
superstitious	To believe in ideas and fears of mysterious things.
trireme	A warship with three rows of oars on each side.
venom	Poison from animals such as snakes or spiders.

Further Information and Web Sites

Books

Ancient Greece: An Interactive History Adventure
by William Caper
(Capstone Press, 2010)

Hail! Ancient Greeks
by Jen Green
(Crabtree Publishing, 2010)

Life in Ancient Times: How The Ancient Greeks Lived
by John Malam
(Gareth Stevens Publishing, 2010)

Web Sites

For Web resources related to the subject of this book, go to: http://www.windmillbooks.com/weblinks and select this book's title.

Places to Visit

The Getty Villa Malibu, Pacific Palisades, CA

The Art Institute of Chicago, Chicago, IL

Author Note

I studied ancient Greek at school, so I had to learn their alphabet and can still remember how to write the letters (just!). The Greeks really were a great people and their legacy is still all around us in the words we use, designs and buildings, and ideas and inventions. But I remember being surprised by some things I learned at school, like the fact that the lovely, white marble sculptures that decorated the Parthenon were once garishly painted! And there are some even bigger surprises in this book about the Greeks!

Jillian Powell

Index

Answers

Page 9 What is it? Athletes doing the long-jump carried weights like this in each hand to help them jump farther.

Page 9 True or false? True. Athletic games were held at the funerals of very rich or important people.

Page 13 True or false? True. Slaves had to get their master or mistresses' permission even to go to the bathroom!

Page 16 What is it? A model of an ear, left as an offering to the gods in thanks for curing a hearing problem.

Page 20 True or false? True. In Greek myth, Hercules killed his enemies by dipping his arrows in poisonous venom.

Page 21 What is it? Spartans wore sticks with their names tied to their arms so their bodies could be identified if they died in battle.

Page 27 What is it? To vote "yes" or "no" on a jury, the ancient Greeks put white or black pebbles into a bowl to be counted.